# MY FIRST BOOK
# DINOSAURS

by Dougal Dixon and Dee Phillips

# MY FIRST BOOK OF DINOSAURS

Copyright © ticktock Entertainment Ltd 2008
First published in Great Britain in 2008 by ticktock Media Ltd.,
Unit 2, Orchard Business Centre, North Farm Road, Tunbridge Wells, Kent, TN2 3XF

ISBN 978 1 84696 653 8 pbk
Printed in China

A CIP catalogue record for this book is available from the British Library.
All rights reserved. No part of this publication may be reproduced, copied, stored in a retrieval system or transmitted in any form or by any means electronic, mechanical, photocopying, recording or otherwise without prior written permission of the copyright owner.

Picture Credits:

(t=top, b=bottom, c=centre, l=left, r=right, OFC=outside front cover, OBC=outside back cover)

John Alston:OFCtc, 3b, 21b, 23b, 27t, 37cr, 41r, 50b, 51r, 48c, 56cl, 59tr, 60cl, 62cl, 65tr, 67, 79bl, 81b, 83t, 85b, 86b, 88b, 90, 94, 95, 96. Lisa Alderson: OFCtl. 2, 24-25, 26-27, 28b, 29, 33, 36-37, 52-53c, 52b, 73, 76-77. Leonella Calvettii: 54-55. Dinosaur Isle, Isle of Wight: 11b. Philip Hood: 17t, 19b. Ian Jackson: 8, 9, 10. Layne Kennedy/ Corbis: 7t. Simon Mendez: OFCcl, 1, 4-5, 8-9, 12c, 13, 15, 17b, 19t, 20-21c, 22-23, 30-31, 31t, 32b, 33t, 46b, 46-47, 48-49c, 50-51c, 57, 58-59c, 61, 62-63, 70cl, 70c, 80-81, 86-87, 88-89, 92-93, 92b. Bob Nicholls: 64-65, 90-91. National Museum of Wales: 70cr. Natural History Museum (De Agostini): 55t. Louie Psihoyos/ Corbis: 6, 7b, 11t. Pulsar EStudio: 18-19main. Luis Rey: OFC main, OFCtr, OFCcr, 14c, 16-17, 38r, 38-39,40-41, 42-43, 44-45, 60b, 68-69, 71, 74-75c, 78, 79r, 82-83, 84-85. Shutterstock: 16t (both), 56b, 72cr, 72cl, 76, 93t. ticktock Media Archive: 35c, 66, 69, 72b, 73, 93b.

# CONTENTS

| | |
|---|---|
| Dinosaur days | 4 |
| How do we know? | 6 |
| Making a fossil | 8 |
| Finding a fossil | 10 |
| Dinosaur food | 12 |
| Reptiles | 14 |
| Dinosaur eggs | 16 |
| Mums and babies | 18 |

### MEET THE CARNIVORES

| | |
|---|---|
| Allosaurus | 20 |
| Tyrannosaurus rex | 22 |
| Giganotosaurus | 24 |
| Compsognathus | 26 |
| Eoraptor | 28 |
| Coelophysis | 30 |
| Deinonychus | 32 |
| Suchomimus | 34 |
| Segnosaurus | 36 |
| Arizonasaurus | 38 |
| Oviraptor | 40 |
| Deinosuchus | 42 |

### MEET THE HERBIVORES

| | |
|---|---|
| Hadrosaurus | 44 |
| Plateosaurus | 46 |
| Diplodocus | 48 |
| Stegosaurus | 50 |
| Sauropelta | 52 |
| Ankylosaurus | 54 |
| Iguanodon | 56 |
| Triceratops | 58 |
| Stygimoloch | 60 |
| Sauroposeidon | 62 |
| Heterodontosaurus | 64 |

### MEET THE FLYING REPTILES

| | |
|---|---|
| Eudimorphodon | 66 |
| Pterodactylus | 68 |
| Dsungaripterus | 70 |
| Dimorphodon | 72 |
| Quetzalcoatlus | 74 |
| Sordes | 76 |
| Archaeopteryx | 78 |

### MEET THE SWIMMING REPTILES

| | |
|---|---|
| Kronosaurus | 80 |
| Elasmosaurus | 82 |
| Ichthyosaurus | 84 |
| Shonisaurus | 86 |
| Cryptoclidus | 88 |
| Liopleurodon | 90 |
| Tylosaurus | 92 |
| Glossary | 94 |
| Index | 96 |

Words that appear in **bold** are explained in the glossary.

# DINOSAUR DAYS

Millions of years ago, the Earth looked very different from today. There were no buildings, no cars and no people. Millions of years ago, the Earth was ruled by huge animals called…

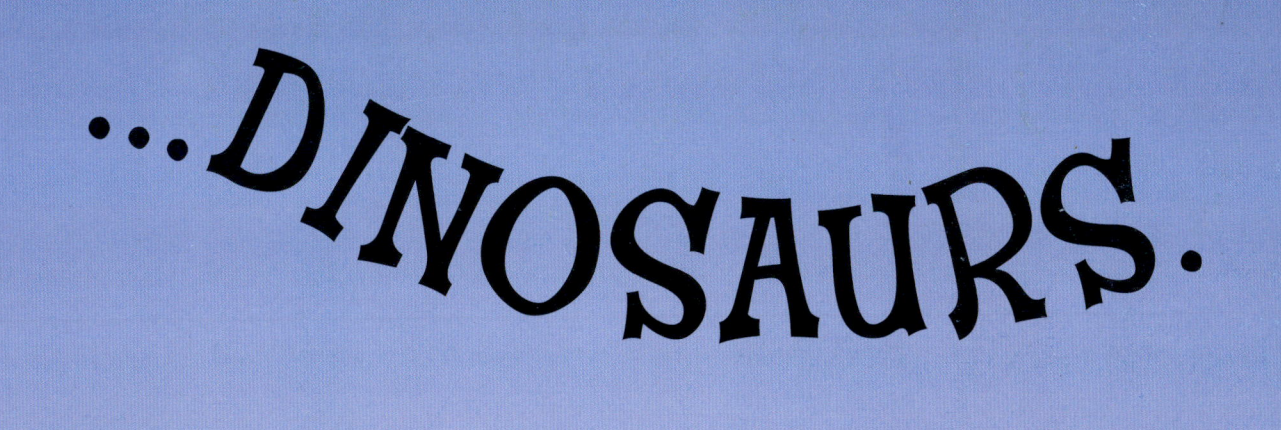

# ...DINOSAURS.

# HOW DO WE KNOW?

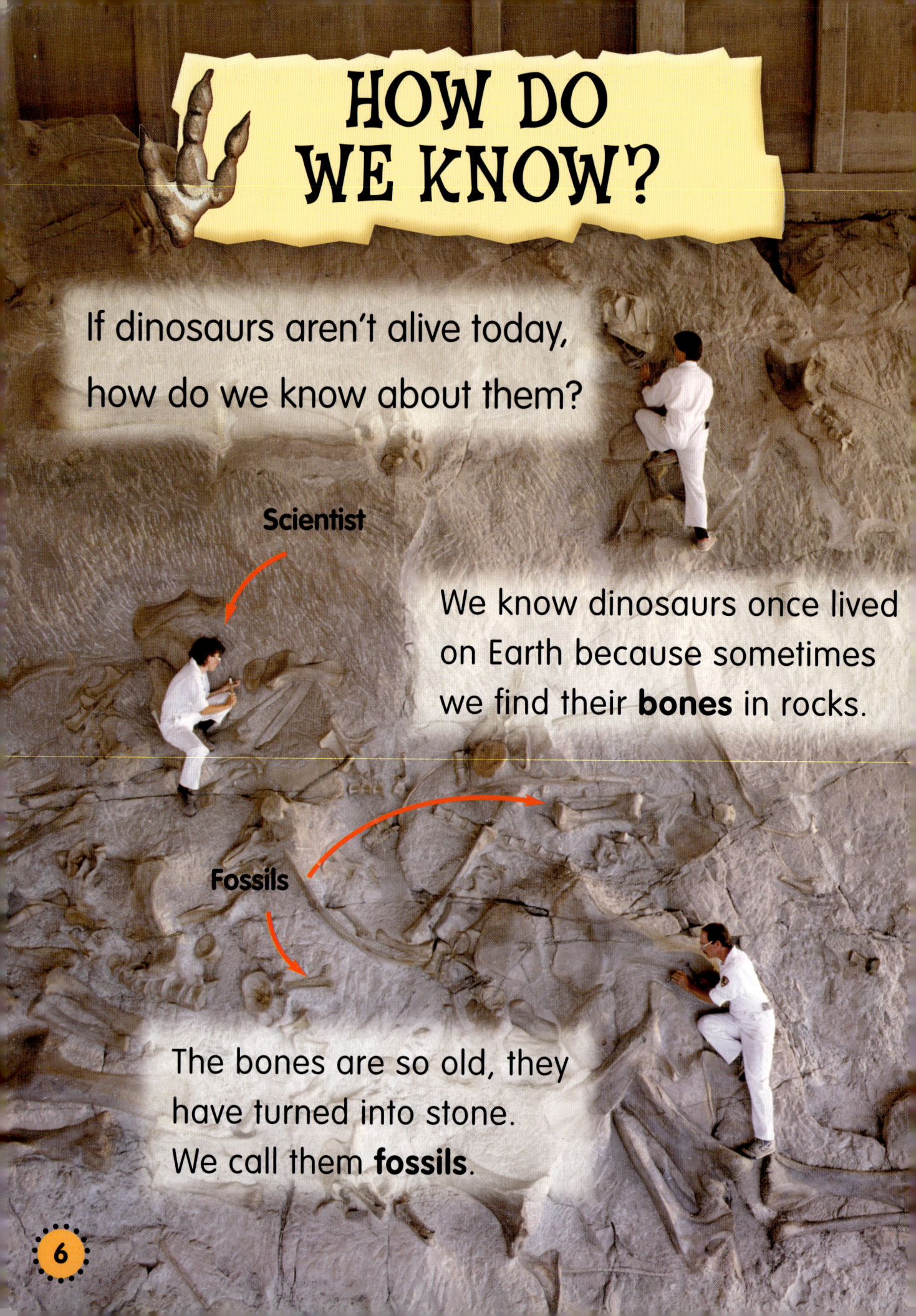

If dinosaurs aren't alive today, how do we know about them?

**Scientist**

We know dinosaurs once lived on Earth because sometimes we find their **bones** in rocks.

**Fossils**

The bones are so old, they have turned into stone. We call them **fossils**.

Finding fossils helps **scientists** work out what dinosaurs looked like and how they lived.

This is a fossil skull from a Tyrannosaurus rex. Look at the teeth. What do you think the teeth tell us about this dinosaur?

**Skull fossil**  **Fossil teeth**  **Rock**

When scientists find a new dinosaur, they give it a name. They use a very old language called **Latin**. Tyrannosaurus rex means "King of the tyrant lizards" in Latin.

**Footprint**

Sometimes we find dinosaur footprints in rocks.

# MAKING A FOSSIL

Let's look at how a dinosaur called Hypsilophodon turned into a **fossil**.

Hypsilophodon was a small dinosaur that ate plants.

Hypsilophodon

One day a Hypsilophodon fell into a lake. It couldn't escape from the water.

The Hypsilophodon drowned and its body fell to the bottom of the lake.

Other animals in the lake ate the Hypsilophodon's skin.

# WHAT HAPPENED NEXT?

# FINDING A FOSSIL

Hypsilophodon's **bones** lay on the bottom of the lake for many, many years.

Mud and sand covered the bones.

Millions of years went by. The bones turned into stone.

# HYPSILOPHODON WAS NOW A FOSSIL.

After millions of years the ground moved. One day, a **scientist** spotted a rock with a **fossil** in it.

The scientist dug up the fossil. He worked out that the fossil was Hypsilophodon.

**Hypsilophodon fossil**

# DINOSAUR FOOD

Dinosaurs can be split into two groups, **herbivores** and **carnivores**.

Herbivores ate plants. They walked on four legs and most of them were very big.

Look out for this picture in your book. It tells you the dinosaur was a herbivore.

Carnivores ate meat and fish. They had sharp teeth. They walked about on two legs killing other animals.

Look out for these pictures in your book. They will tell you the dinosaur was a carnivore.

# REPTILES

Dinosaurs belonged to a group of animals called **reptiles**. All sorts of other reptiles lived at the same time as the dinosaurs.

Flying reptiles had furry bodies and leathery wings.

The reptiles were **carnivores**. They ate meat, fish or **shellfish**.

Swimming reptiles had legs like **paddles**. They lived in the sea.

Look for these pictures in your book. They will tell you what kind of food the animal ate.

# DINOSAUR EGGS

Dinosaurs laid eggs – just like birds and snakes do.

Some dinosaur eggs were as **big** as a football. Some were smaller than a golf ball.

Some dinosaurs sat on their eggs to keep them warm.

Big, heavy dinosaurs did not sit on their eggs. They might break them!

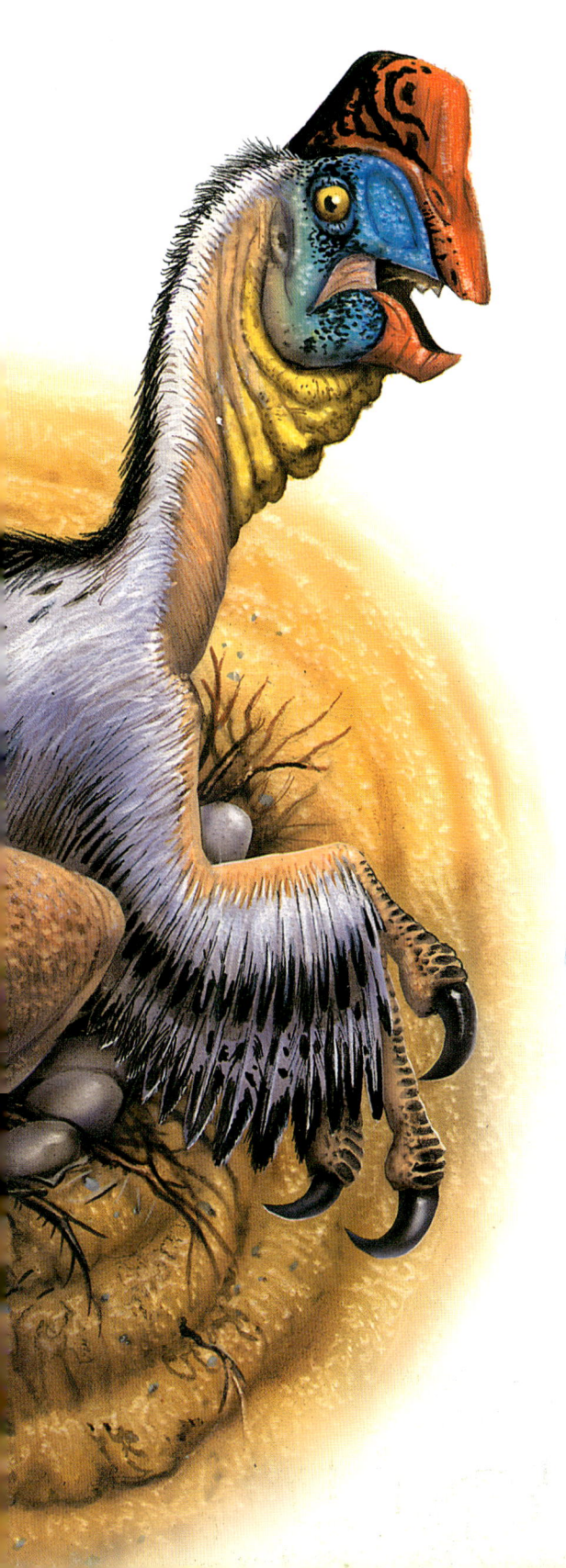

They hid their eggs in a pile of leaves to keep them warm and safe.

Some **reptiles** dug a hole for their eggs.

# MUMS AND BABIES

Some dinosaur mums looked after their babies. They kept their babies safe from danger.

Triceratops mums fought with **carnivores** who wanted to eat their babies.

Triceratops

Some baby plant-eating dinosaurs ate leaves and twigs. They had to learn to find the plants they liked.

**Tyrannosaurus**

Baby meat-eating dinosaurs had to learn to hunt.

# MEET THE CARNIVORES

Allosaurus was a big, meat-eating dinosaur.

Allosaurus attacked and ate big plant-eating dinosaurs.

Meat-eating dinosaurs had small arms. Allosaurus had three **claws** on each hand to grip its **prey**.

Allosaurus had over 70 sharp teeth.

Claws

# ALLOSAURUS

**Scientists** have found lots of Allosaurus **fossils**. That's how we know how big it was.

## SIZE CHART

9 metres long

Allosaurus means "A different lizard".

# TYRANNOSAURUS REX

Tyrannosaurus rex may have been the heaviest meat-eating dinosaur. It weighed the same as an elephant.

Sometimes we call this dinosaur T. rex.

**Scientists** are not sure if T. rex hunted other animals or if it ate animals that were already dead.

## CARNIVORES

T. rex had a good sense of smell. It could smell a dead animal from kilometres away.

T. rex could fit an animal as big as a cow into its mouth, whole!

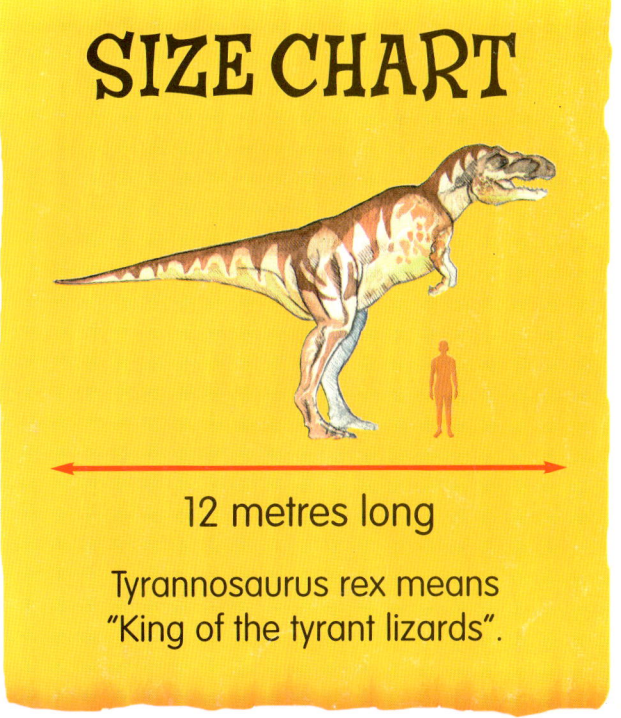

### SIZE CHART

12 metres long

Tyrannosaurus rex means "King of the tyrant lizards".

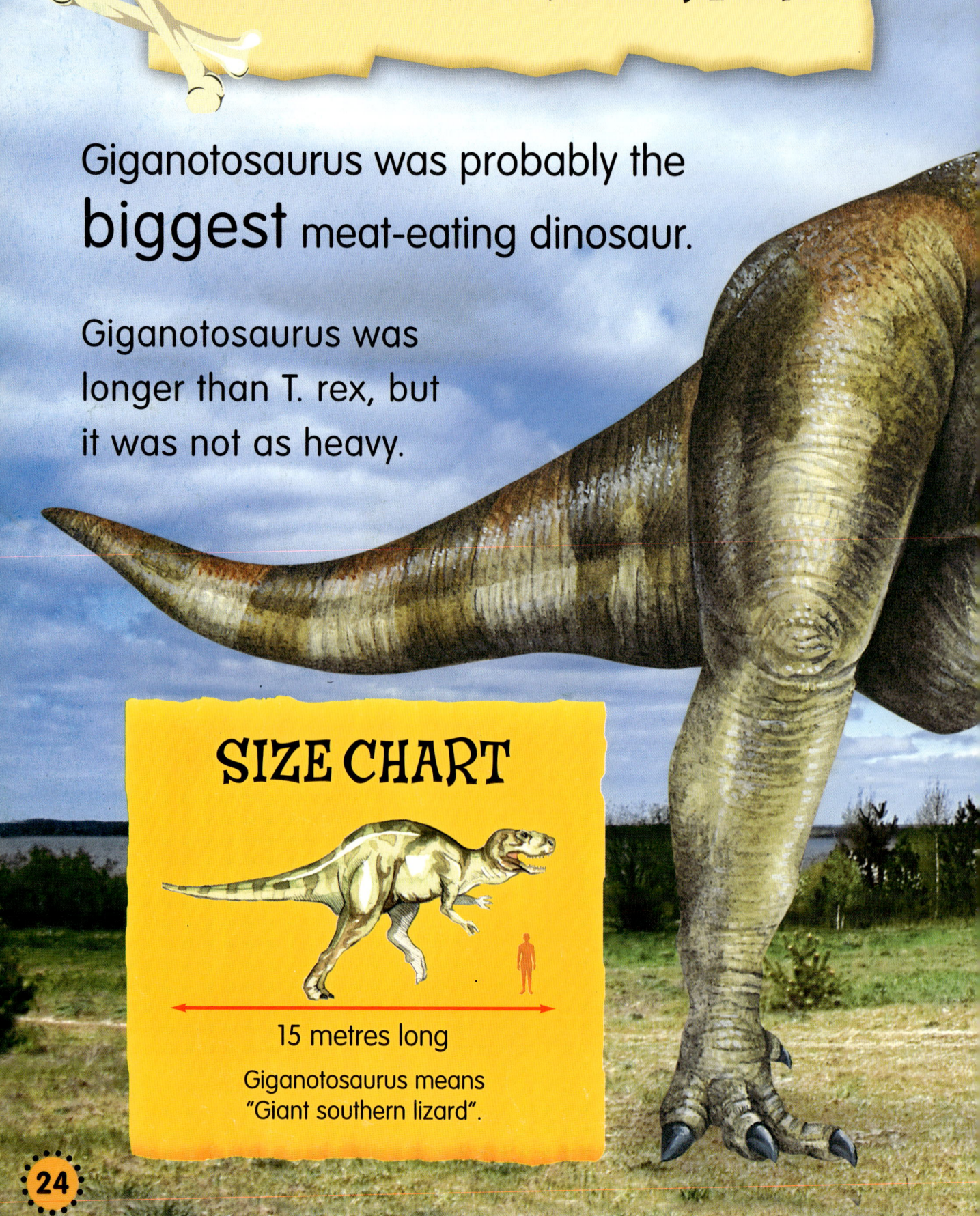

# GIGANOTOSAURUS

Giganotosaurus was probably the **biggest** meat-eating dinosaur.

Giganotosaurus was longer than T. rex, but it was not as heavy.

### SIZE CHART

15 metres long

Giganotosaurus means "Giant southern lizard".

**CARNIVORES**

It had **jaws** that could **swallow** you whole!

Jaws

Some of its teeth were 15 centimetres long!

**Scientists** have not yet found many **fossils** of Giganotosaurus. So, they are not quite sure what it really looked like.

25

# COMPSOGNATHUS

Compsognathus was one of the smallest dinosaurs. Its body was the size of a chicken.

Compsognathus was tiny, but it was a fierce hunter.

Its long legs show that Compsognathus was a fast runner.

CARNIVORES

## SIZE CHART

90 centimetres long

Compsognathus means " Pretty jaw".

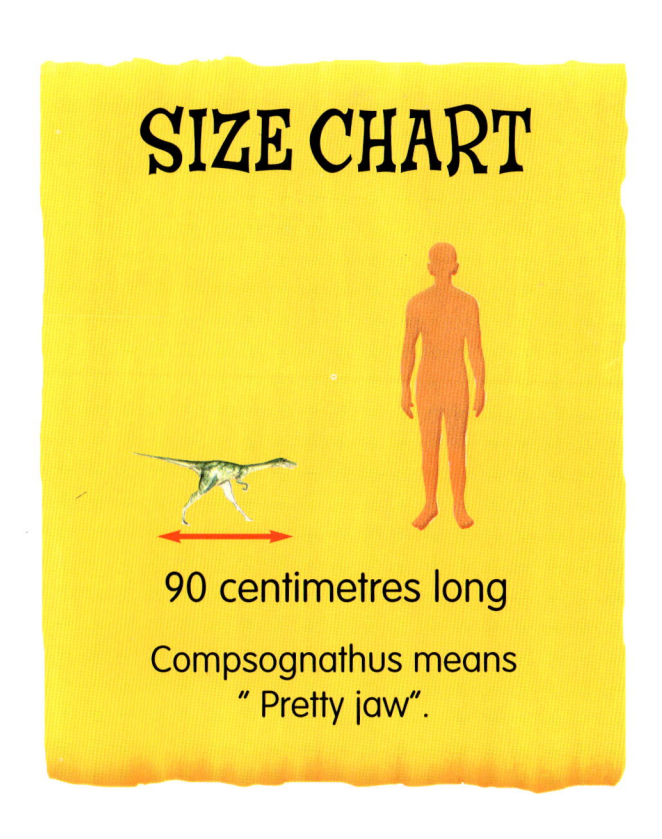

This dinosaur's long tail helped it to balance when it was running.

**Lizard**

Compsognathus ate **lizards**. We know this because **scientists** have found lizard **fossils** in the stomach of a Compsognathus fossil. Scientists think it ate **insects**, too.

# EORAPTOR

Eoraptor was one of the first dinosaurs to live on Earth. It was a tiny **carnivore** about the size of a fox.

Eoraptor lived millions of years before Allosaurus and T. rex. However, it had the same body shape as the big meat-eaters who came after it.

## SIZE CHART

1 metre long

Eoraptor means "Early hunter".

CARNIVORES

This fast, fierce little dinosaur hunted for **lizards** and **insects**.

It had five fingers on each hand for grabbing **prey**.

# COELOPHYSIS

**Scientists** think that Coelophysis lived in **packs** or in family groups.

Scientists think this because they found a whole group of Coelophysis **fossils** in one place. This showed the animals had lived and died together.

CARNIVORES

Coelophysis hunted for **lizards** and smaller dinosaurs.

### SIZE CHART

3 metres long

Coelophysis means "Hollow form".

Coelophysis had long legs. It was a fast runner.

# DEINONYCHUS

Deinonychus was a fierce dinosaur with very big **claws**. It could run very fast after its **prey**.

**Scientists** think that Deinonychus hunted in **packs**.

They would gather around their prey.

They would slash it with their sharp claws.

# CARNIVORES

## SIZE CHART

4 metres long

Deinonychus means "Terrible claw".

Deinonychus had a big brain, so scientists think it was quite clever.

Claw

33

# SUCHOMIMUS

Suchomimus was a huge, strong dinosaur that lived by rivers.

Claw

## CARNIVORES

Suchomimus used its **claws** to hook fish out of the water and throw them onto the land. Then it snapped them up in its long **jaws**.

### SIZE CHART

11 metres long

Suchomimus means "Crocodile mimic".

Suchomimus was a huge **predator**. But there were even bigger creatures in rivers, such as giant crocodiles!

# SEGNOSAURUS

Segnosaurus was one of the strangest looking dinosaurs!

When **scientists** found Segnosaurus **fossils**, they found it hard to work out what it looked like.

Scientists think it was covered in feathers like a bird.

**Short legs**

**CARNIVORES**

Segnosaurus is still a bit of a mystery. But scientists think it had rounded shoulders and big hips.

It also had long arms and short legs, like a gorilla or chimpanzee.

### SIZE CHART

6 metres long

Segnosaurus means "Slow lizard".

Segnosaurus had huge **claws**. Maybe they were for digging into **insects'** nests.

# ARIZONASAURUS

Arizonasaurus was a kind of crocodile that lived on land. Arizonasaurus lived just before the time of the dinosaurs. It lived in the **desert** and hunted for plant-eating **reptiles**, like **lizards**.

## SIZE CHART

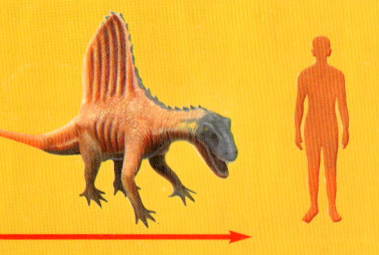

3 metres long

Arizonasaurus means "Lizard from Arizona".

Arizonasaurus didn't crawl like a crocodile. It had straight legs and walked more like a dog.

# CARNIVORES

Arizonasaurus had a sail on its back. The sail could store heat from the Sun. This helped to keep Arizonasaurus warm.

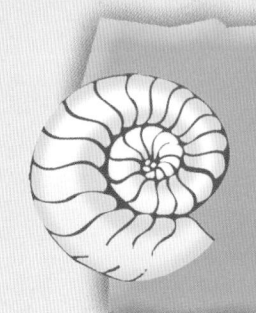

# OVIRAPTOR

Oviraptor was a dinosaur that looked and acted like a bird. **Scientists** think it even had feathers!

Scientists found a **fossil** of an oviraptor sitting on a nest. It had its wings spread over some eggs.

This showed the scientists that oviraptor sat on its eggs until they **hatched**.

Oviraptor could flap its wings, but it couldn't fly.

# CARNIVORES

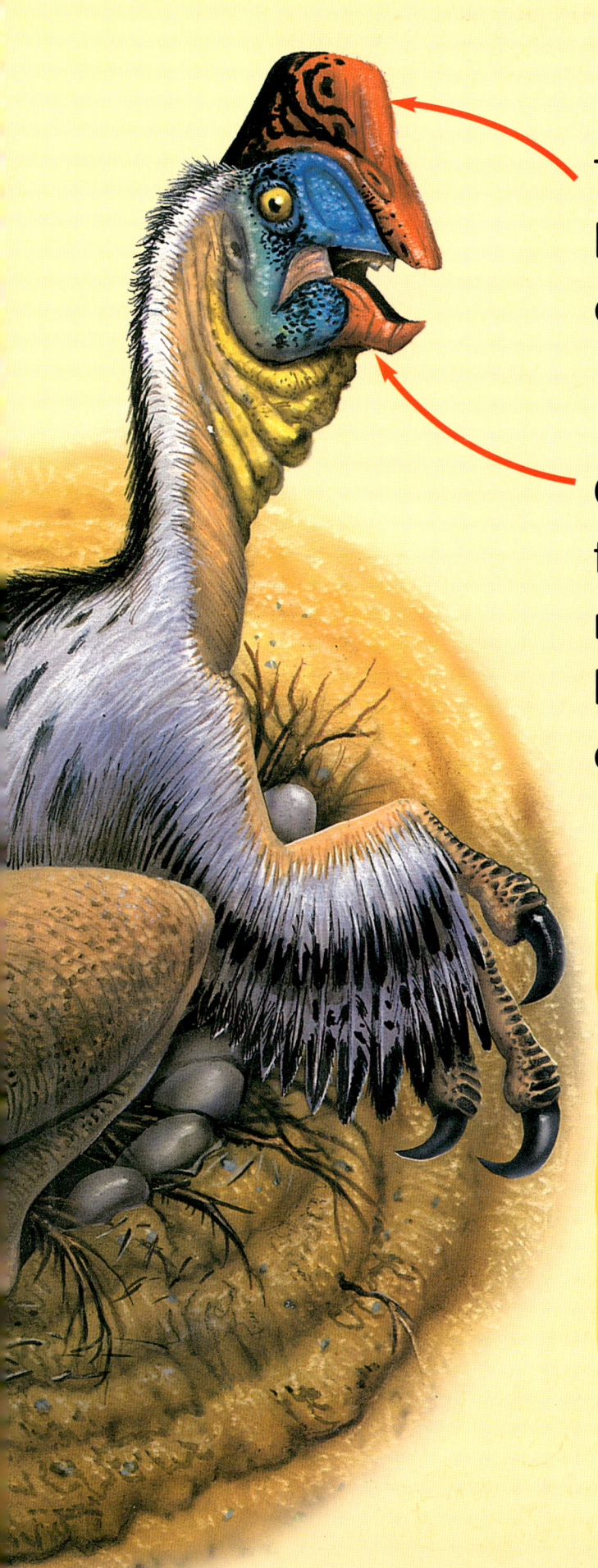

This **crest** might have been used to signal to other Oviraptors.

Oviraptor had a beak and two teeth on the roof of its mouth. Its strong **jaws** may have been used for crushing snails or **shellfish**.

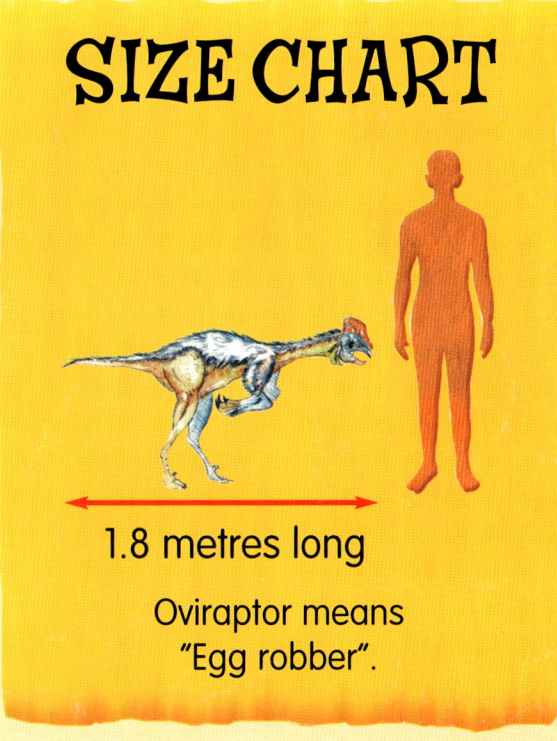

## SIZE CHART

1.8 metres long

Oviraptor means "Egg robber".

# DEINOSUCHUS

Deinosuchus was a giant crocodile that lived at the time of the dinosaurs. It was the BIGGEST crocodile ever to have lived on Earth.

Even though it lived 70 million years ago, Deinosuchus looked the same as modern-day crocodiles.

### SIZE CHART

15 metres long
Deinosuchus means "Terrible crocodile".

CARNIVORES

Deinosuchus was large enough to catch and kill big dinosaurs.

It waited in lakes and rivers for its **prey** to come for a drink – then it attacked!

Its powerful tail helped it speed through water.

# MEET THE HERBIVORES

Hadrosaurus was one of the "duck-billed" dinosaurs. We call them that because they had mouths that looked a bit like duck beaks.

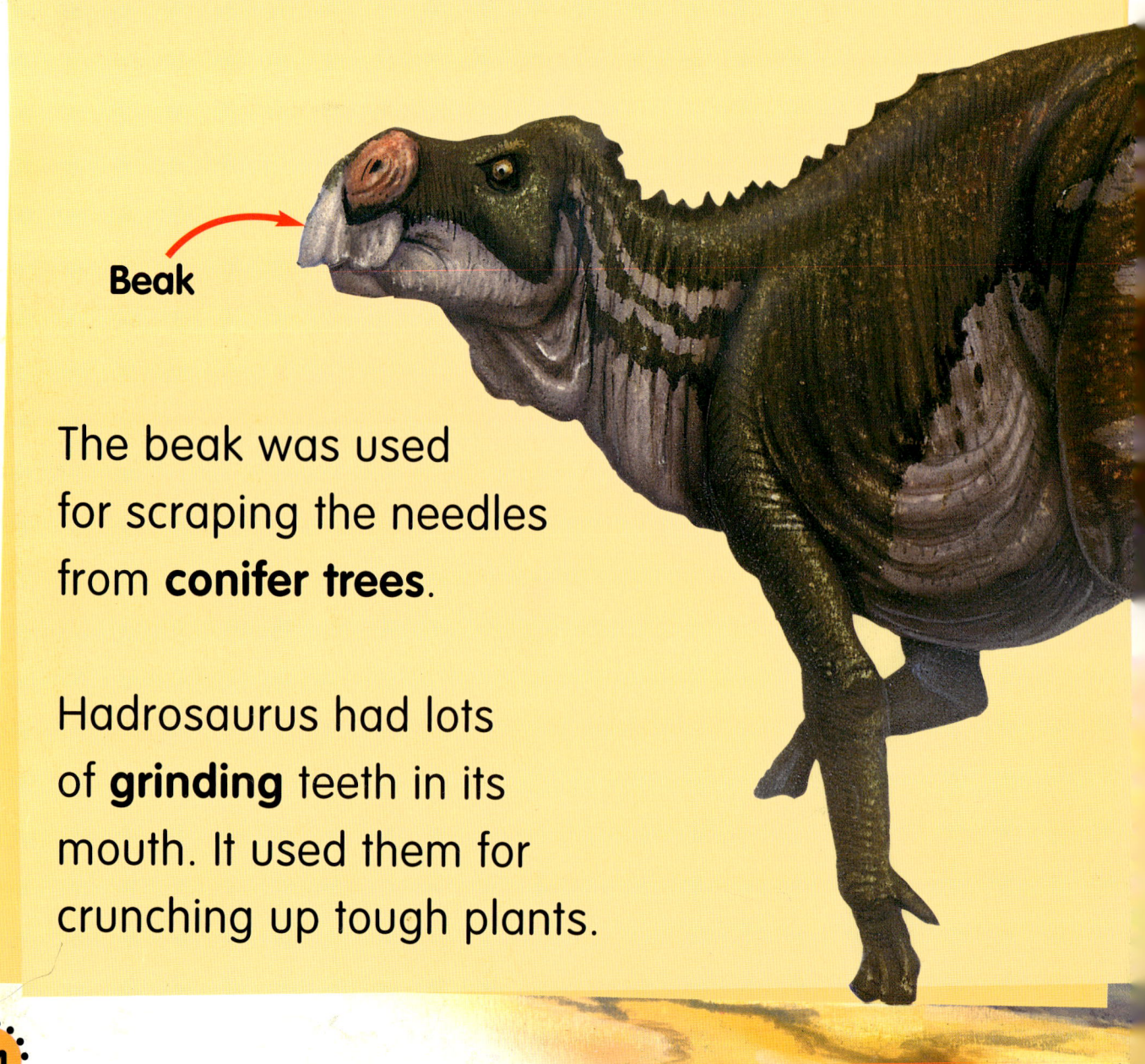

**Beak**

The beak was used for scraping the needles from **conifer trees**.

Hadrosaurus had lots of **grinding** teeth in its mouth. It used them for crunching up tough plants.

# HADROSAURUS

Its long tail helped it to balance when it walked on two legs.

**SIZE CHART**

7 metres long
Hadrosaurus means "Sturdy lizard".

# PLATEOSAURUS

Plateosaurus was one of the first dinosaurs to be discovered by **scientists**. Some Plateosaurus **fossils** were found in France in 1837.

## SIZE CHART

7 metres long

Plateosaurus means "Flat lizard".

# HERBIVORES

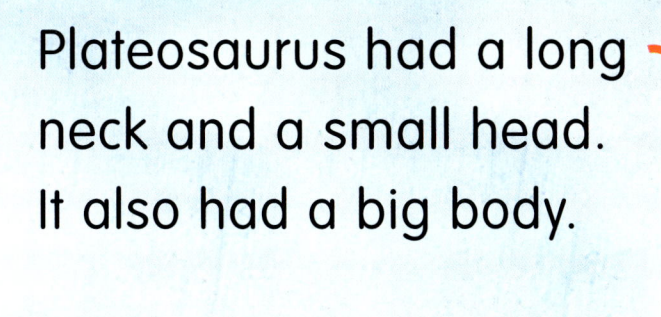

Plateosaurus had a long neck and a small head. It also had a big body.

Plants are tough to **digest**. So plant-eating dinosaurs needed lots of **intestines** to digest their food.

Plant-eating dinosaurs had big bodies so there was room for their long intestines and big stomachs.

# DIPLODOCUS

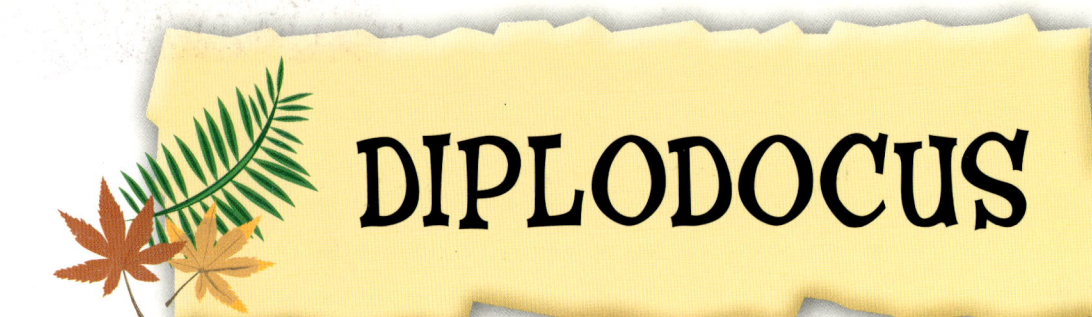

The biggest dinosaurs of all were the **sauropods**. They were **herbivores** with long necks. Diplodocus was a sauropod.

### SIZE CHART

27 metres long

Diplodocus means "Double beamed".

Diplodocus ate ferns from the ground and leaves from trees.

HERBIVORES

Diplodocus walked on all fours. But sometimes it would rise up on its back legs to eat from trees.

Diplodocus was so big, it had to keep eating all the time!

To help **grind** up food in its stomach, it swallowed stones.

It used its long tail like a whip, to keep **predators** away.

# STEGOSAURUS

Some **herbivores** had special body parts to protect them from **predators**. Stegosaurus had plates on its back.

**Plates**

Stegosaurus also had **spikes** on its tail. It used them to fight off **carnivores**!

## SIZE CHART

7 metres long
Stegosaurus means "Covered lizard".

**HERBIVORES**

**Scientists** have found **fossils** of Stegosaurus plates, but they don't know for sure how they were arranged.

### HERE ARE SOME IDEAS:

Flat on the back | In pairs

In a single row | In a double row

Maybe they could even be pointed towards a predator!

# SAUROPELTA

Some plant-eating dinosaurs were covered in **armour**, like battle tanks!

Sauropelta was a big, heavy, armoured dinosaur. It weighed the same as three elephants.

## SIZE CHART

5 metres long

Sauropelta means "Shielded lizard".

**HERBIVORES**

A **predator** would break its teeth on Sauropelta's armour! The only way to hurt this dinosaur was to flip it over.

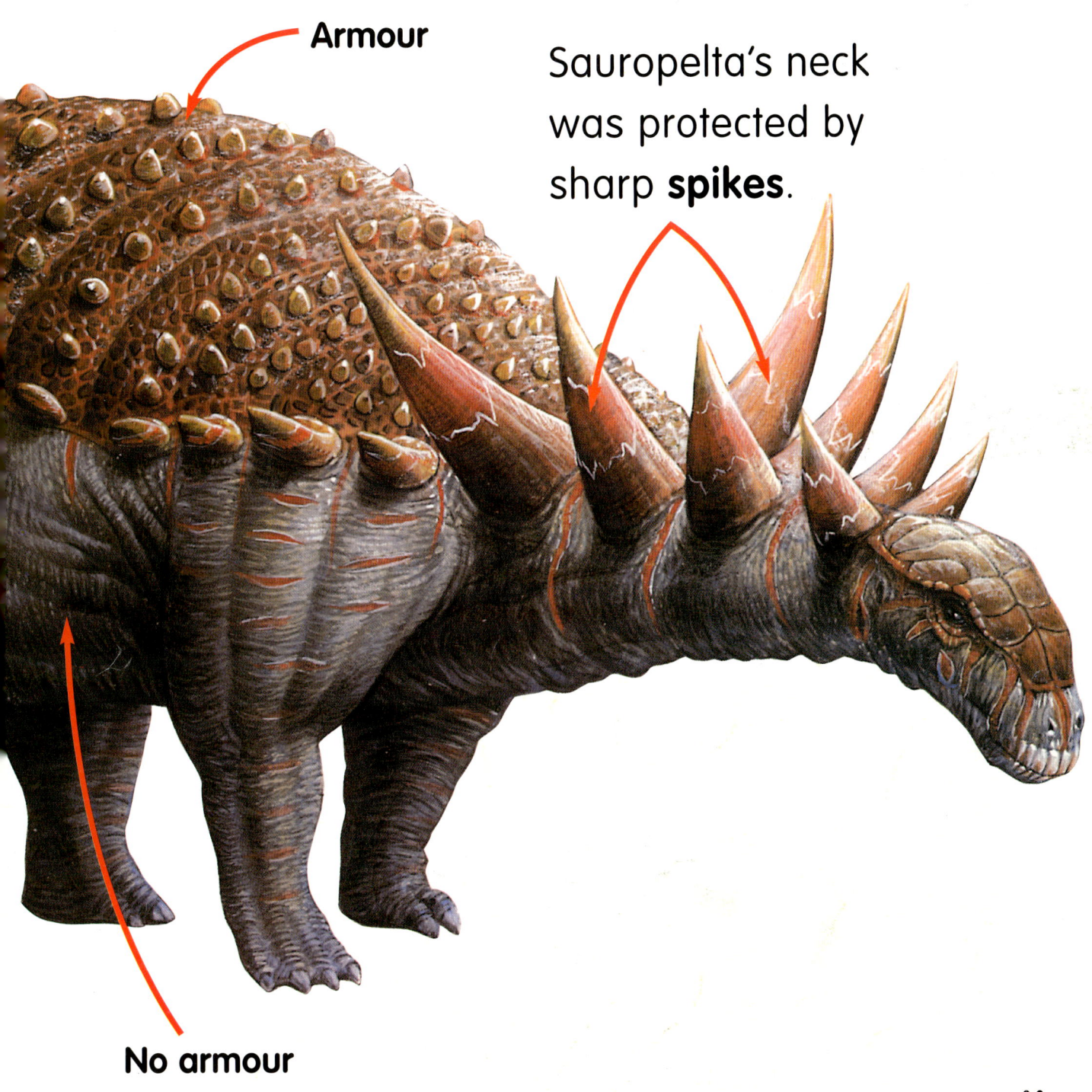

Armour

Sauropelta's neck was protected by sharp **spikes**.

No armour

53

# ANKYLOSAURUS

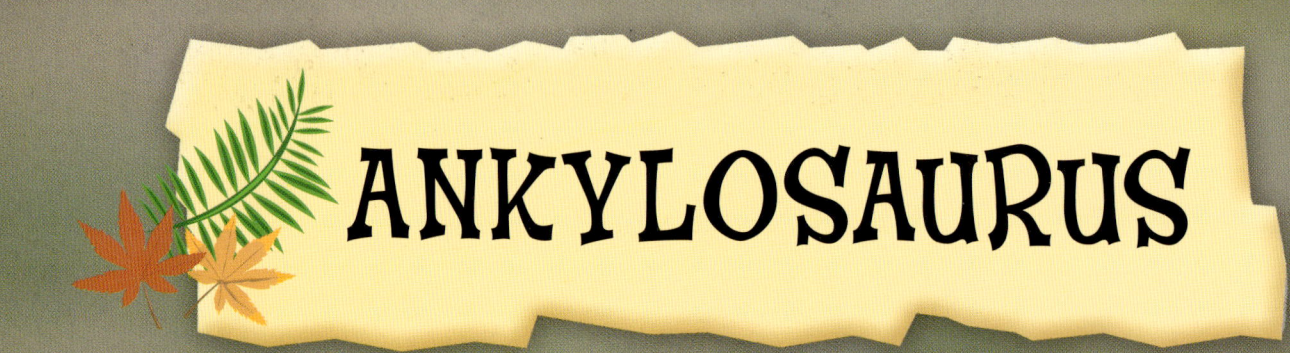

Ankylosaurus was the biggest of the armoured dinosaurs.

Ankylosaurus had a heavy club on its tail. The club was made from chunks of **bone**.

It could swing the club like a weapon at **predators**.

HERBIVORES

## SIZE CHART

11 metres long

Ankylosaurus means "Fused lizard".

Its back was covered in **armour**.

Even its head was protected by hard, bony armour.

55

# IGUANODON

Iguanodon was one of the first dinosaurs to be discovered.

**SIZE CHART**

10 metres long
Iguanodon means "Iguana-toothed".

At first, **scientists** thought they had found **fossils** from a fish or a hippopotamus. But then they realised they had found something new – a dinosaur!

Iguanodon was a bit like a modern-day iguana – only much BIGGER!

**Iguana**

# HERBIVORES

Iguanodons lived in **herds**. They moved from one area to another to find **reeds** to eat.

Herd

# TRICERATOPS

Some **herbivores** had **horns** on their heads. Triceratops had three horns. It also had a frill of **bone** to protect its neck. Triceratops lived in large **herds**.

Horns

Frill

Triceratops had a strong beak for pulling at plants.

HERBIVORES

If a **predator** attacked the herd, the **adults** formed a circle with their horns facing outwards. The babies were safe in the middle of the circle.

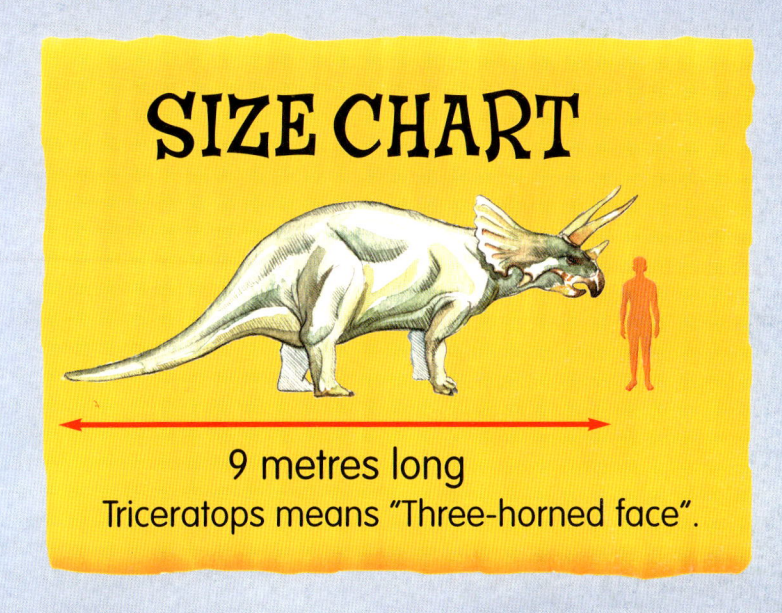

### SIZE CHART

9 metres long
Triceratops means "Three-horned face".

# STYGIMOLOCH

Stygimoloch came from a group of dinosaurs that **scientists** call the "boneheads".

## SIZE CHART

2.7 metres long

Stygimoloch means "Horned devil from the river of death".

Stygimoloch had a huge lump of **bone** in its head. Males used this for head-butting other males in fights over **mates**.

It also had **horns** around its head to scare away **predators**.

60

**HERBIVORES**

61

# SAUROPOSEIDON

Sauroposeidon was the tallest animal ever to have lived on Earth!

**SIZE CHART**

30 metres long

Sauroposeidon means "Lizard earthquake god".

Sauroposeidon was 21 metres tall – that's the same as four giraffes standing on top of each other!

**HERBIVORES**

So far, **scientists** have only found four neck **fossils** from this dinosaur. They used these fossils to work out its size.

Sauroposeidon possibly weighed the same as 60 elephants!

Its neck was 15 metres long.

# HETERODONTOSAURUS

Heterodontosaurus looked like a fierce **carnivore**, but it was actually a small **herbivore**.

Tusks

It had nipping teeth inside its beak and **tusks** at the side. At the back of its **jaws** it had **grinding** teeth for crunching up plants.

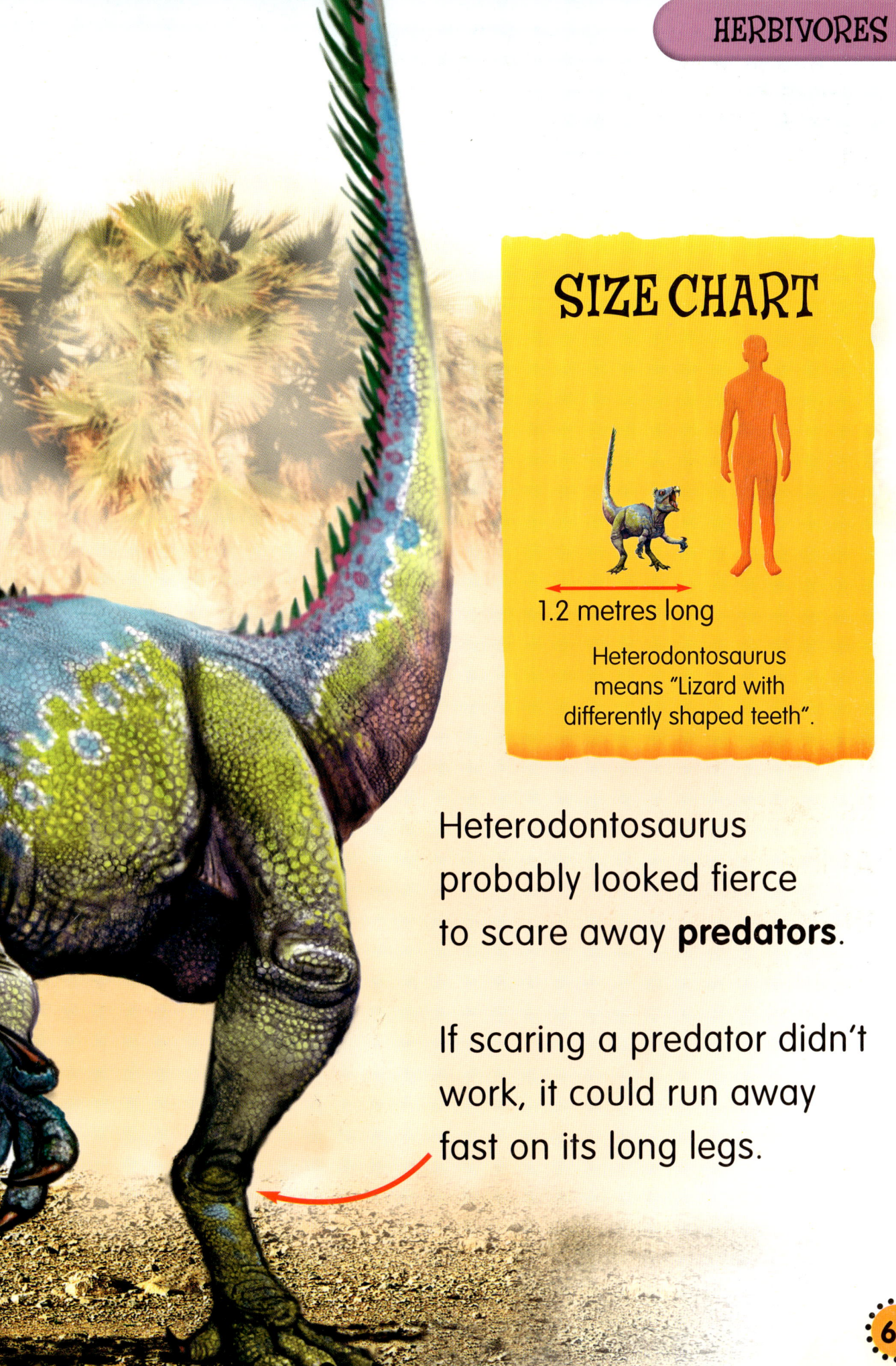

### HERBIVORES

## SIZE CHART

**1.2 metres long**

Heterodontosaurus means "Lizard with differently shaped teeth".

Heterodontosaurus probably looked fierce to scare away **predators**.

If scaring a predator didn't work, it could run away fast on its long legs.

65

# MEET THE FLYING REPTILES

At the time of the dinosaurs, flying bird-like **reptiles** lived on Earth.

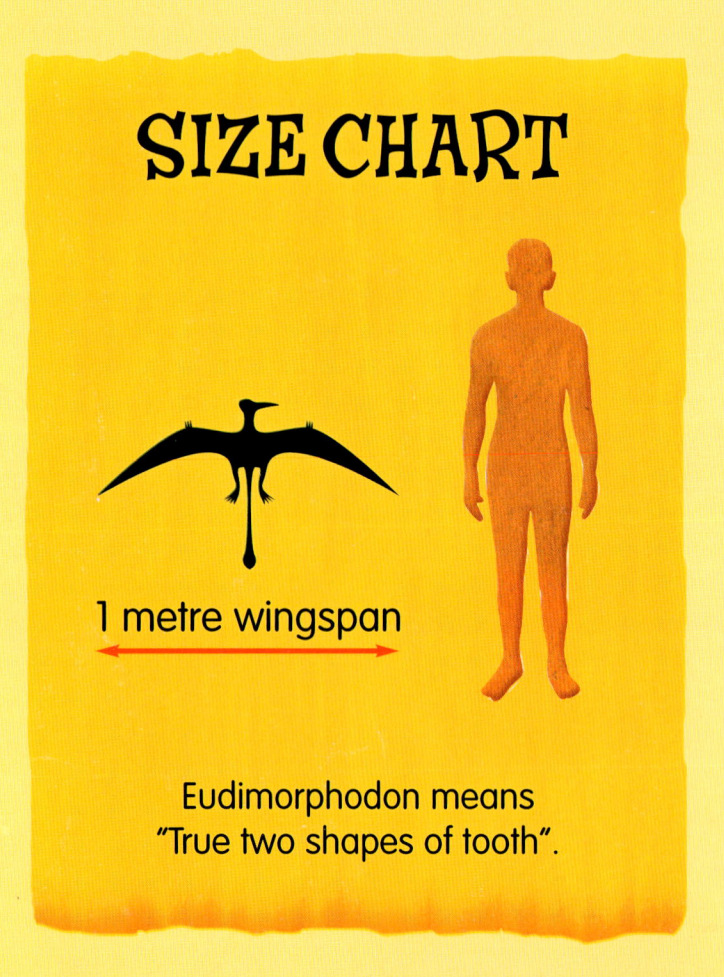

## SIZE CHART

1 metre wingspan

Eudimorphodon means "True two shapes of tooth".

One group of flying reptiles were called the **pterosaurs**. Eudimorphodon was a pterosaur.

Eudimorphodon lived about 225 million years ago.

A **paddle**-shaped flap on its tail helped Eudimorphodon to steer.

# EUDIMORPHODON

Eudimorphodon had two types of teeth. One type for spearing fish, and one for chewing them.

**Spearing teeth**

Pterosaurs didn't have feathers like birds, they had furry bodies.

67

# PTERODACTYLUS

Pterodactylus was a member of the **pterosaur** family. Some Pterodactylus were tiny – just the size of a modern-day starling. They ate **insects**.

Pterodactylus had a long fourth finger on each hand.

Some types of Pterodactylus were bigger – the size of modern-day eagles. They ate fish or small **lizards**.

FLYING REPTILES

Pterodactylus had a short tail, a furry body and wings made of skin.

The long finger made a kind of frame for the wing.

## SIZE CHART

Some were the size of starlings.

Some were the size of eagles.

Pterodactylus means "Wing finger".

69

# DSUNGARIPTERUS

Just like some modern-day birds, some flying **reptiles** had **crests** on their heads. They used them to signal to each other.

**Pteranodon**   **Tapejara**   **Tupuxuara**

## SIZE CHART

3 metre wingspan

Dsungaripterus means "Wing from Junggar in China".

Dsungaripterus **fossils** were the first **pterosaur** fossils to be found in China.

FLYING REPTILES

Dsungaripterus probably ate **shellfish**.

**Crest**

Its pointed **jaws** could dig shellfish out of little holes in rocks.

It had tooth-like knobs at the back of its mouth. These would have been able to crush the shells.

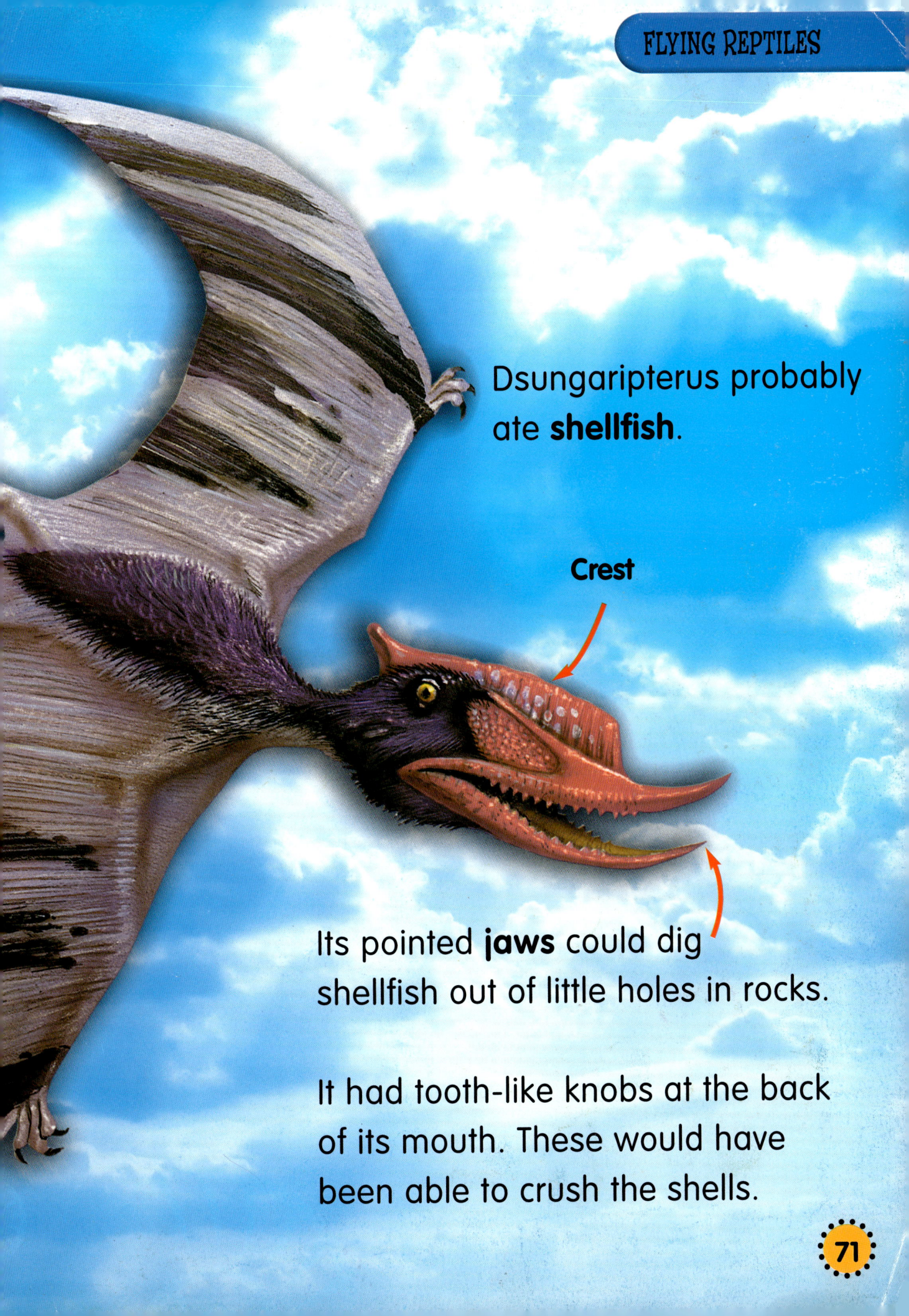

# DIMORPHODON

Dimorphodon was a **pterosaur** with a big beak. **Scientists** think the beak might have been colourful like a modern-day toucan.

**Dimorphodon**   **Toucan**

Dimorphodons might have used their beaks for signalling to each other.

## SIZE CHART

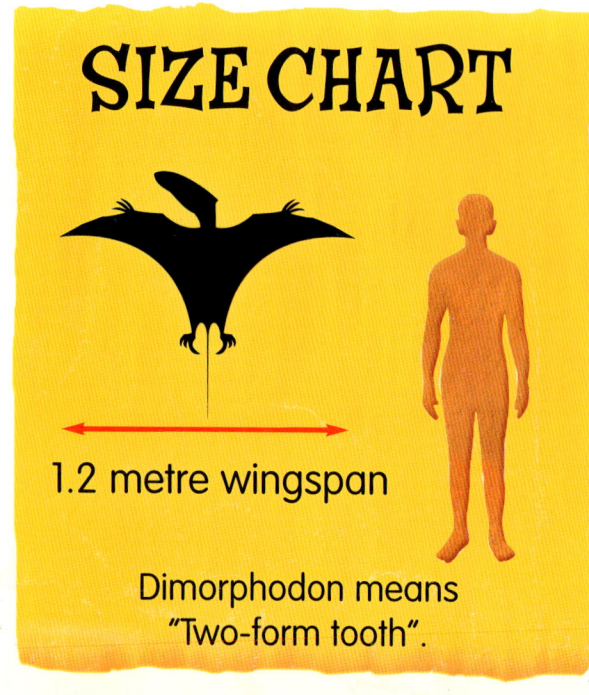

1.2 metre wingspan

Dimorphodon means "Two-form tooth".

**FLYING REPTILES**

Scientists have used **fossil** footprints to work out how Dimorphodons walked.

They have found footprints that show four sets of tracks.

This means they walked on their back legs and used their arms like walking sticks.

# QUETZALCOATLUS

Quetzalcoatlus was the biggest of the flying **reptiles**. It was the size of a small plane!

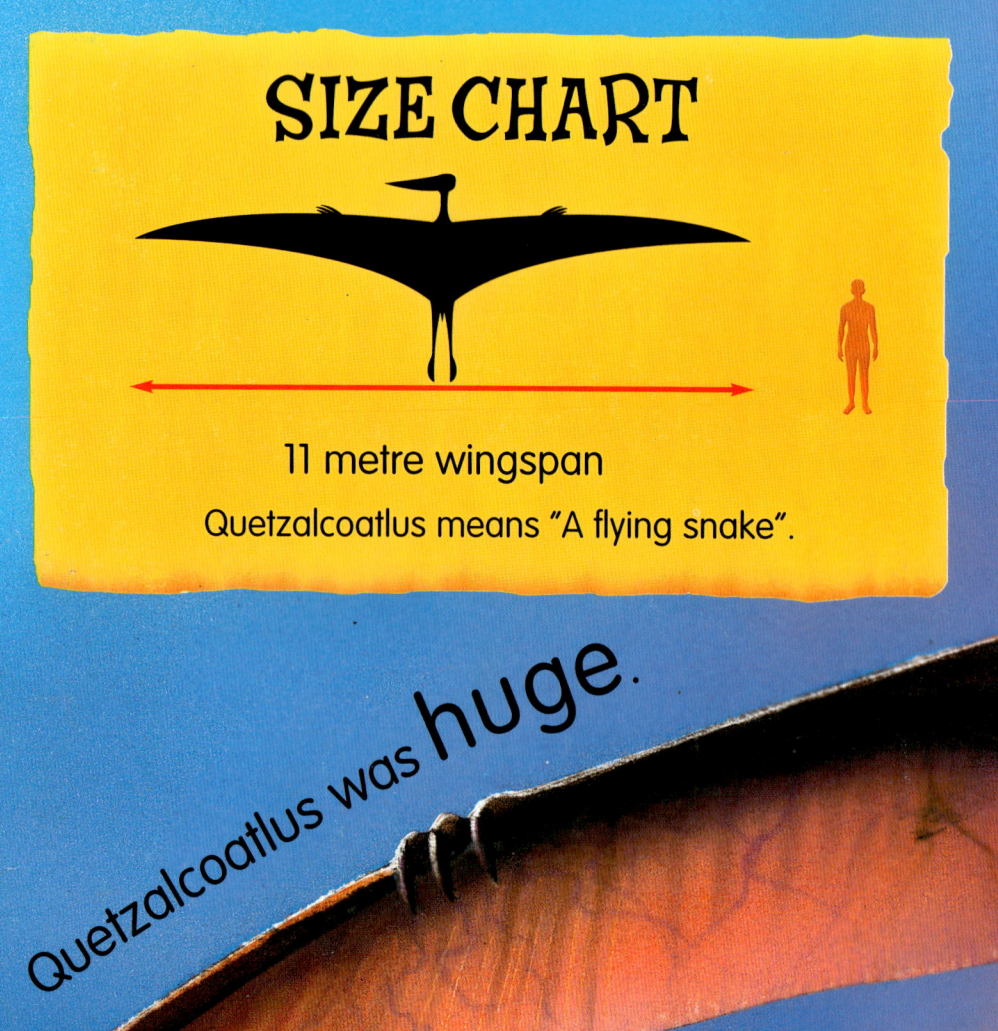

## SIZE CHART

11 metre wingspan

Quetzalcoatlus means "A flying snake".

Quetzalcoatlus was huge.

Its body was light so it could stay in the air. It probably only weighed the same as one and a half humans.

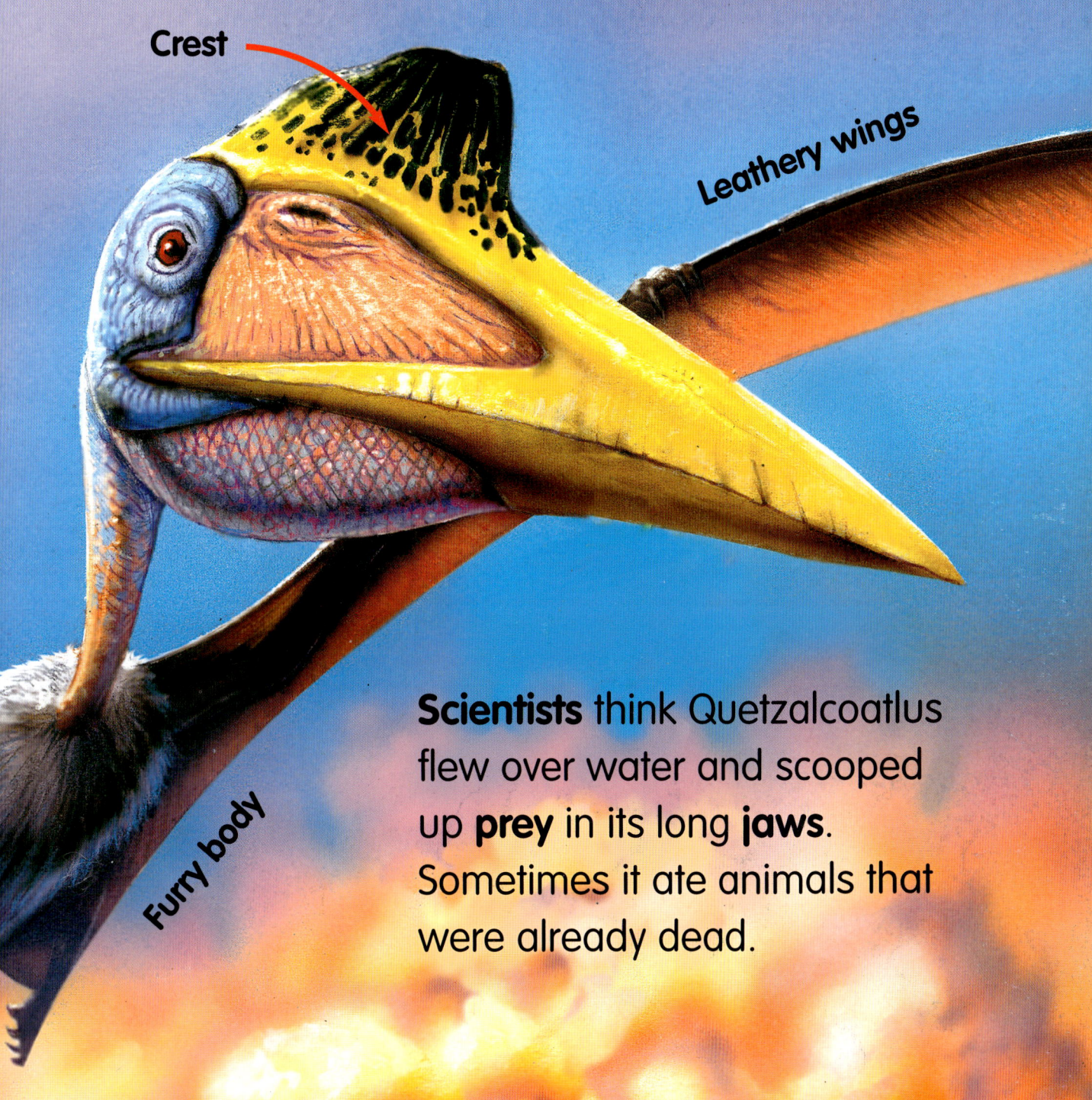

FLYING REPTILES

Crest

Leathery wings

Furry body

**Scientists** think Quetzalcoatlus flew over water and scooped up **prey** in its long **jaws**. Sometimes it ate animals that were already dead.

Quetzalcoatlus had good eyesight to see prey far below it.

75

# SORDES

Sordes was a small **pterosaur** that lived about 150 million years ago.

A long stiff tail

A paddle for steering

In many ways, pterosaurs had bodies more like modern-day bats than birds.

Leathery wings

Furry body

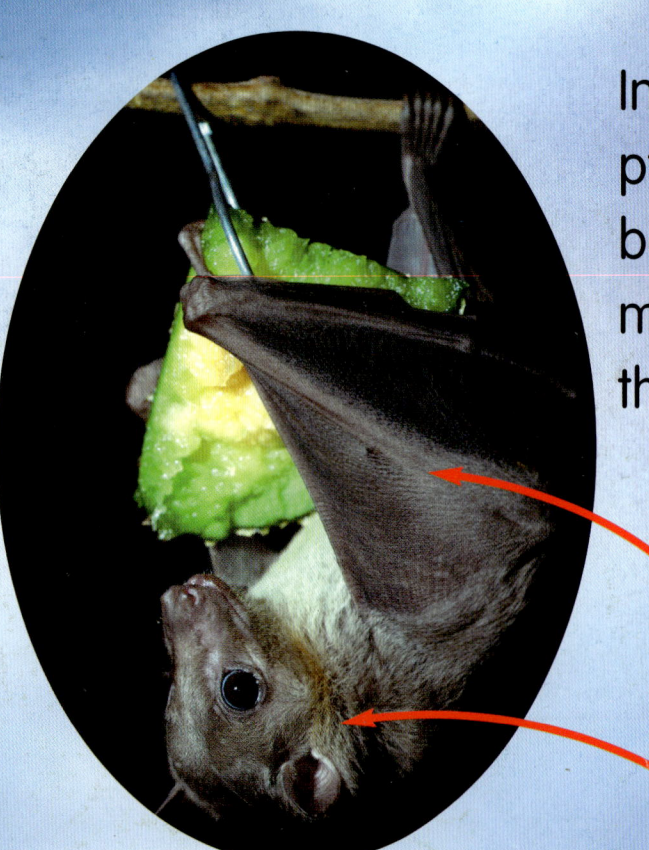

Fruit bat

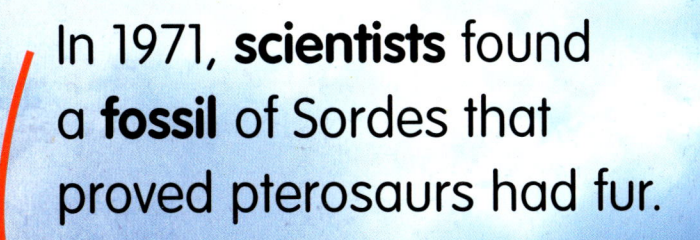

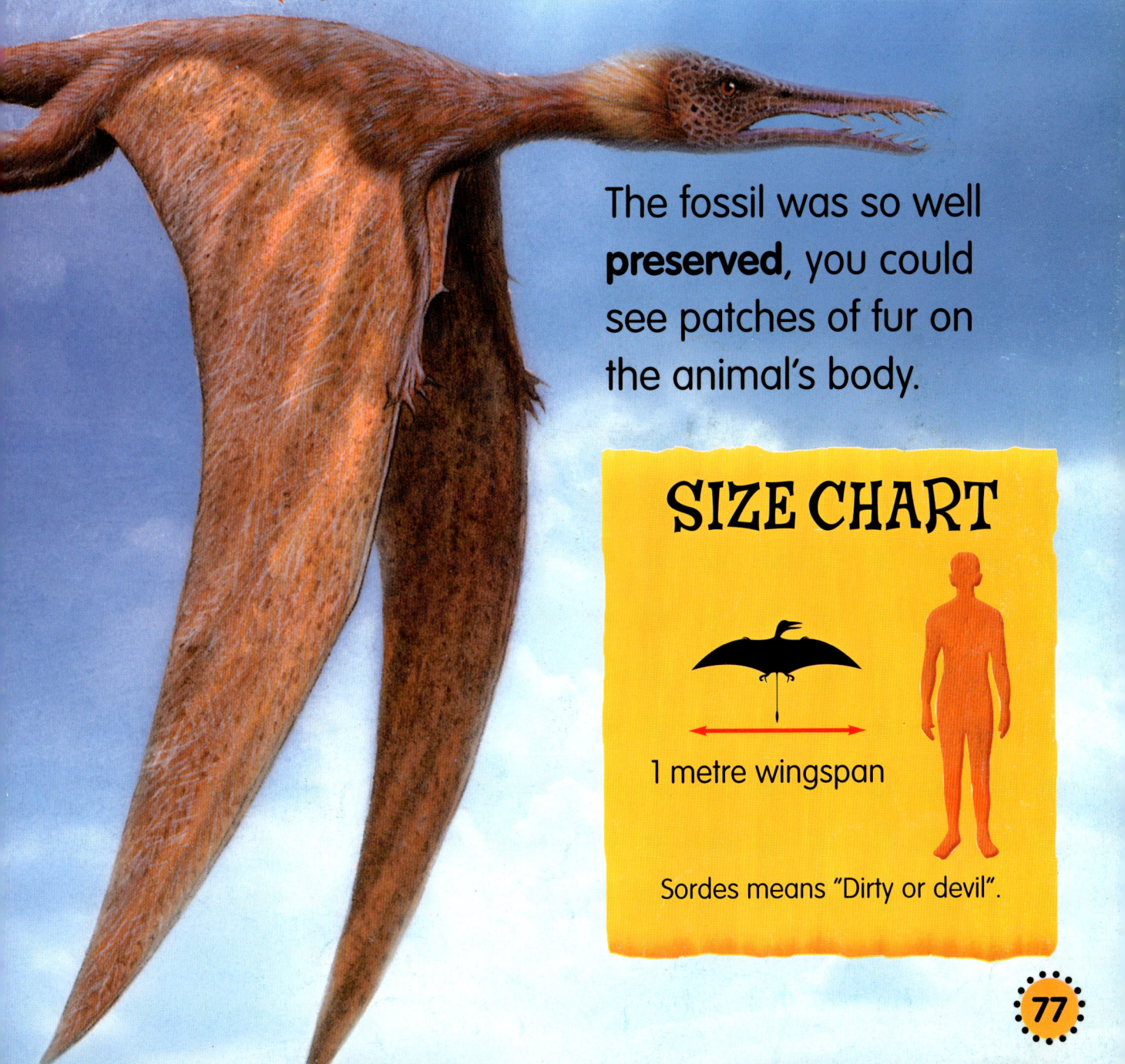

**FLYING REPTILES**

In 1971, **scientists** found a **fossil** of Sordes that proved pterosaurs had fur.

The fossil was so well **preserved**, you could see patches of fur on the animal's body.

## SIZE CHART

1 metre wingspan

Sordes means "Dirty or devil".

# ARCHAEOPTERYX

Archaeopteryx was the first ever bird to live on Earth. This little animal proved that, over millions of years, dinosaurs **evolved** into birds.

**Scientists** realised this because Archaeopteryx was like a bird in some ways, and like a dinosaur in others.

It had **jaws** and teeth like a dinosaur. It ate **insects**.

It had feathers like a bird.

FLYING REPTILES

It had **claws** like a dinosaur.

## SIZE CHART

It was the size of a pigeon.

Archaeopteryx means "Ancient wing".

**Feathers**

# MEET THE SWIMMING REPTILES

At the time of the dinosaurs, giant swimming **reptiles** lived in the sea.

Kronosaurus looked a bit like a modern-day whale.

A smooth body for gliding through water.

It swam like a modern-day turtle, paddling with its four **flippers**.

# KRONOSAURUS

Kronosaurus had a short neck and a head that was nearly 3 metres long!

Sharp teeth

It probably fed on **shellfish**, **octopus** and giant **squid**.

It gets its name from Kronos, a giant in stories from **ancient Greece**.

### SIZE CHART

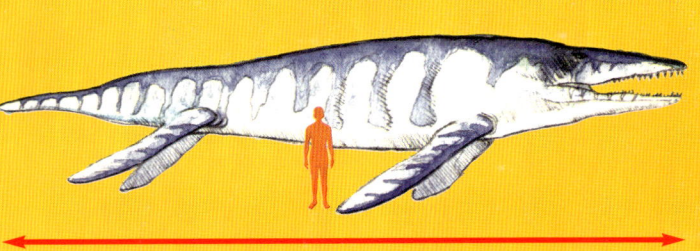

15 metres long

Kronosaurus means "Kronos lizard".

# ELASMOSAURUS

Elasmosaurus was a giant swimming **reptile** with a very long neck.

It swam using its **paddles** in a flying motion. Modern-day sea lions swim like this.

Its neck was...

## SWIMMING REPTILES

### SIZE CHART

14 metres long

Elasmosaurus means "Long lizard".

It had a small head and lots of sharp teeth.

...over 7 metres long!

As it swam along, it could use its long neck to reach out and grab fish.

83

# ICHTHYOSAURUS

Ichthyosaurus was a small swimming **reptile**. It looked a bit like a shark or a dolphin.

Fin

Tail

Paddle

Ichthyosaurus had a tail like a fish, a shark-like **fin** on its back and **paddles** for legs.

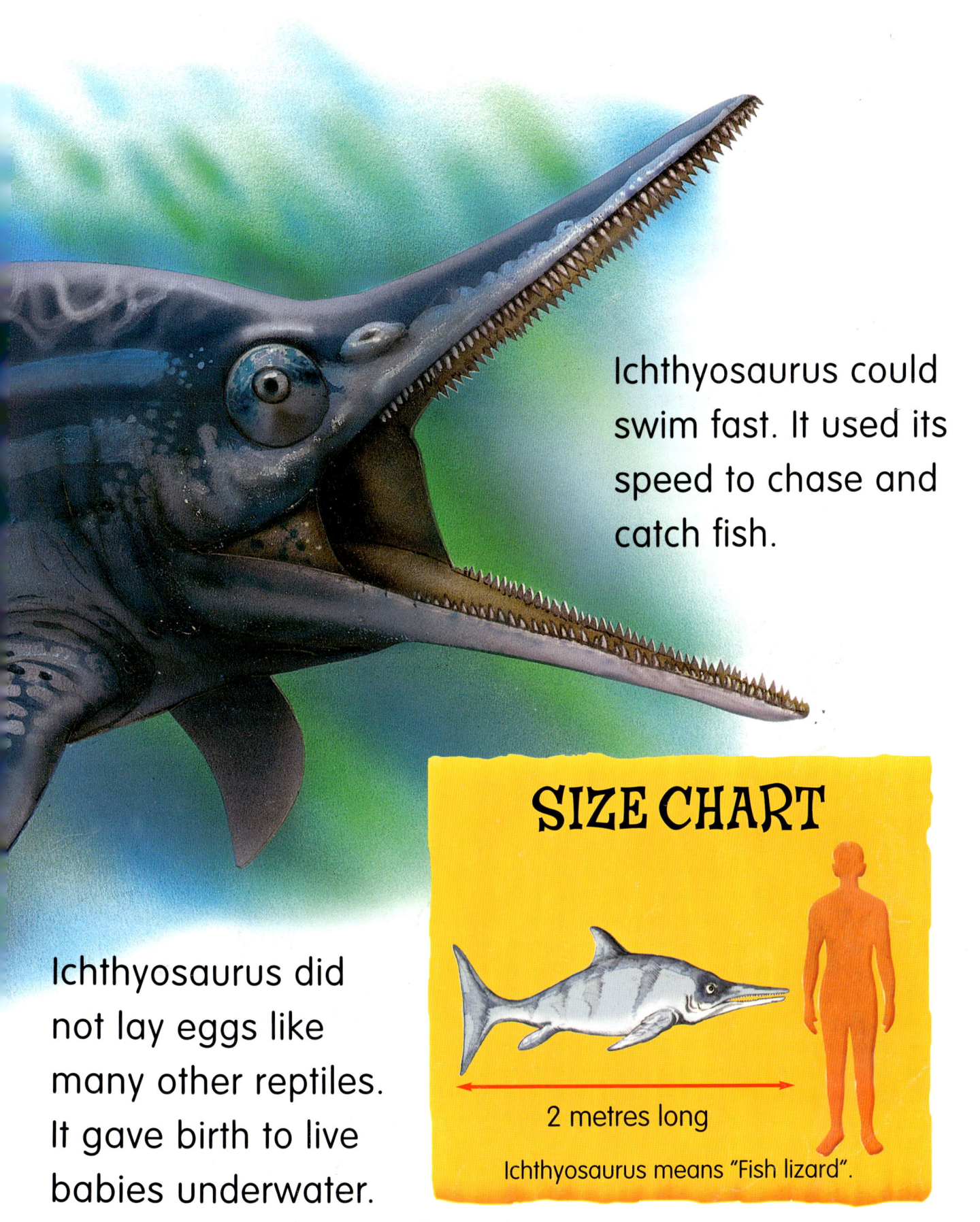

SWIMMING REPTILES

Ichthyosaurus could swim fast. It used its speed to chase and catch fish.

Ichthyosaurus did not lay eggs like many other reptiles. It gave birth to live babies underwater.

## SIZE CHART

2 metres long

Ichthyosaurus means "Fish lizard".

# SHONISAURUS

Shonisaurus was the **biggest** member of the **ichthyosaur** family.

**Scientists** found one **fossil** of a Shonisaurus that was 21 metres long! That's nearly as big as a blue whale.

## SIZE CHART

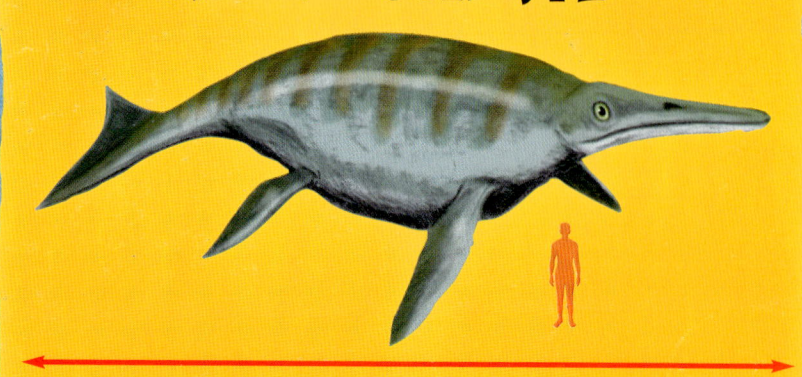

15 metres long

Shonisaurus means "Lizard from the Shoshone Mountains".

# SWIMMING REPTILES

**Fin**

Shonisaurus was a strong swimmer. Its **streamlined** body helped it to move easily through the water.

It had teeth at the front of its snout for grabbing fish.

Big **paddles** for swimming.

# CRYPTOCLIDUS

When Cryptoclidus **fossils** were first discovered, one **scientist** said that Cryptoclidus must have looked like a snake threaded through a turtle.

Cryptoclidus was a type of **plesiosaur**. There were short-necked plesiosaurs and long-necked plesiosaurs.

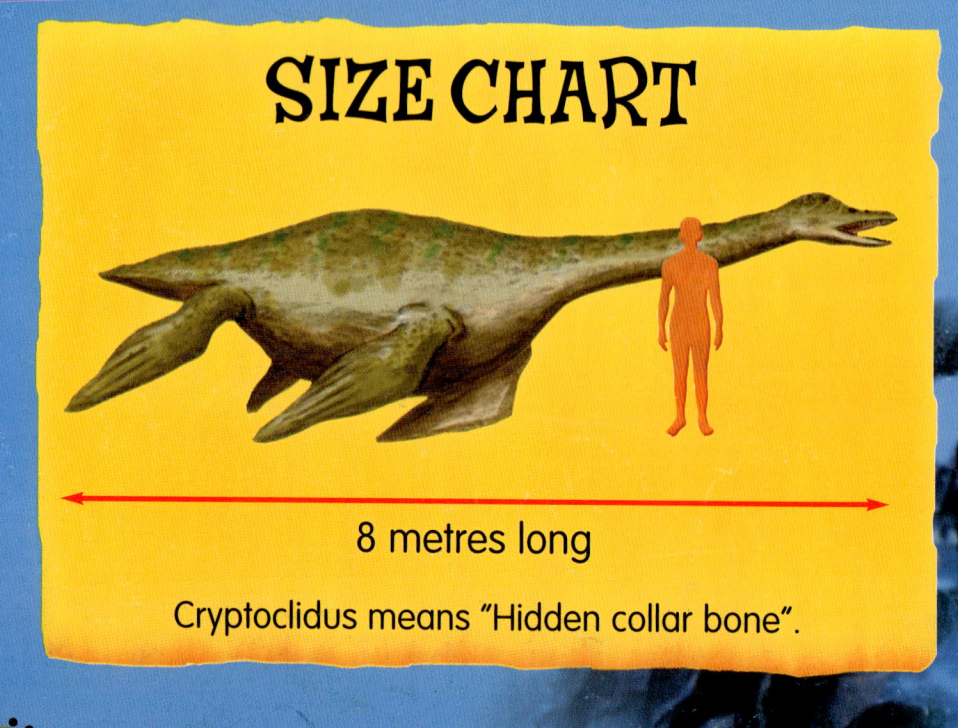

## SIZE CHART

8 metres long

Cryptoclidus means "Hidden collar bone".

SWIMMING REPTILES

Cryptoclidus was a long-necked plesiosaur.

Cryptoclidus ate **squid** and fish. It had long pointed teeth – just right for catching slippery **prey**.

89

# LIOPLEURODON

Liopleurodon was one of the biggest hunters to ever live on Earth. It was a HUGE, short-necked **plesiosaur**.

## SIZE CHART

15 metres long

Liopleurodon means "Smooth-sided tooth".

Liopleurodon would swallow stones to help it sink in the water.

If it wanted to rise up to chase **prey**, it would spit the stones out.

## SWIMMING REPTILES

**Elasmosaurus**

Liopleurodon had teeth that were 20 centimetres long!

**Scientists** have found bite marks from Liopleurodon on **fossils** of large **ichthyosaurs** and plesiosaurs.

# TYLOSAURUS

Tylosaurus was one of a group of swimming **reptiles** called **mosasaurs**. These animals had long bodies and a long tail.

The long, flat tail helped Tylosaurus move fast through water when it was hunting.

## SIZE CHART

14 metres long

Tylosaurus means "Swollen lizard".

SWIMMING REPTILES

**Komodo dragon lizard**

Mosasaur **fossils** show these animals were a lot like modern-day **lizards**. Mosasaurs **evolved** from lizards that lived on Earth 200 million years ago.

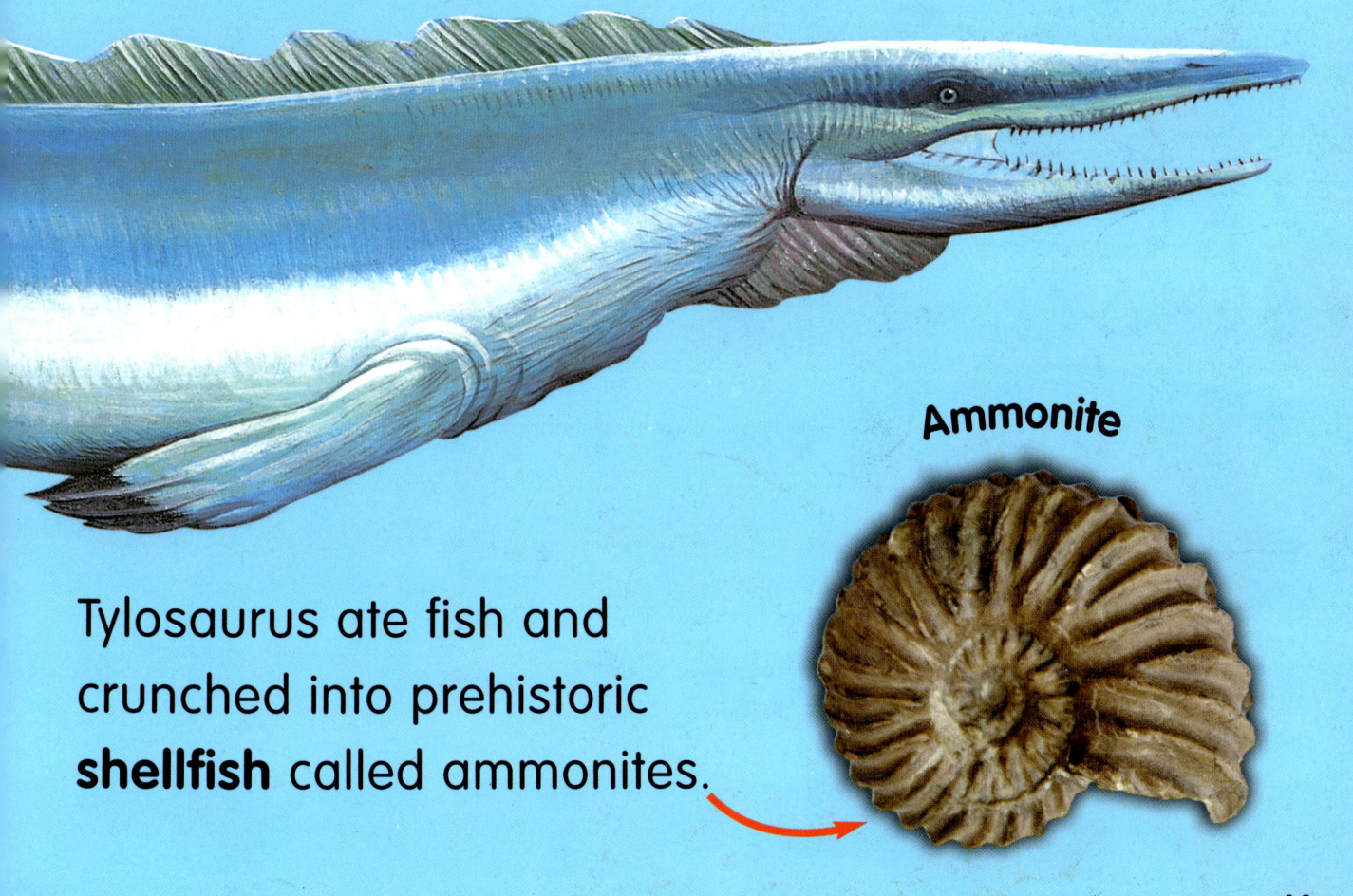

**Ammonite**

Tylosaurus ate fish and crunched into prehistoric **shellfish** called ammonites.

# GLOSSARY

**ancient Greece** The people and country of Greece 2,500 years ago.

**armour** Something hard and tough that protects you. Dinosaur armour was made from bone covered in horn.

**bone** A hard part inside a human or animal's body. Bones make up a body's skeleton.

**carnivore** An animal that only eats meat.

**claw** A long, sharp nail that an animal uses to attack, or to defend itself.

**conifer tree** An evergreen tree with small, tough, needle-like leaves.

**crest** A part of an animal's head that can be a special shape or very colourful.

**desert** A dry place that gets very little rain. Most deserts are sandy.

**digest** To turn food into substances that can be used by the body.

**evolve** To change very slowly over a long time from one type of animal to another.

**fin** A flat, triangle-shaped body part on the back of a water animal. Fins help an animal to move through the water.

**flipper** A flat arm-like body part that water animals use for swimming.

**fossil** A piece of bone or tooth that has turned to stone over millions of years.

**grind** To crush something into small pieces between two hard objects, such as teeth.

**hatch** To break out of an egg.

**herbivore** An animal that only eats plants.

**herd** A group of animals that live together, but are not all one family.

**horn** A tough material like your fingernails. The word horn also means a pointed weapon made of this material on an animal's head.

**ichthyosaur** A reptile that looked like a fish or a dolphin. It lived at the time of the dinosaurs.

**insect** A little animal without a backbone that is covered by a jointed shell. Insects have six legs and some have wings.

**intestines** The long tube from the stomach to the bowel where food is turned into substances that the body can use.

**jaw** The bony framework of the mouth that teeth are attached to.

**Latin** An ancient language from Italy. Scientists use Latin to name animals and plants.

**lizard** A type of reptile that crawls on the ground and usually has short legs and a long tail.

**mate** An animal's partner that it produces babies with.

**mosasaur** A type of giant swimming lizard from the time of the dinosaurs.

**octopus** A sea animal that has eight legs and no skeleton.

**pack** A group of animals that hunt together.

**paddle** A body part that is wide and flat. It can be used by a water animal for swimming.

**plesiosaur** A type of swimming reptile from the time of the dinosaurs. Some plesiosaurs had long necks and small heads. Others had short necks.

**predator** An animal that hunts other animals for food.

**preserved** When something old has stayed in good condition.

**prey** An animal that is hunted as food by a predator.

**pterosaur** A type of flying reptile from the time of the dinosaurs. Pterosaurs had leathery wings supported on a single big finger.

**reed** A type of tough grass that grows by water.

**reptile** A member of a group of egg-laying animals that usually have scales and no hair. Snakes and crocodiles are reptiles.

**sauropod** A member of the group of big, plant-eating dinosaurs with very long necks and tiny heads.

**scientist** A person who uses science to investigate and find things out about the world.

**shellfish** An animal that lives in water and is protected by a shell.

**spike** A sharp, pointed weapon on a dinosaur's body.

**squid** A fast-swimming sea animal with a soft body, eight short arms and two long arms.

**streamlined** Something that has a smooth shape that cuts through air or water easily.

**tusk** A large, pointed tooth.

# INDEX

**A**
Allosaurus 20-21, 28
Ankylosaurus 54-55
Archaeopteryx 78-79
Arizonasaurus 38-39
armour 50-51, 52-53, 54-55

**B**
baby dinosaurs 18-19, 59, 85
birds 36, 40-41, 68, 78-79

**C**
carnivores 12-13, 15 (and see meat-eaters)
claws 20, 32-33, 34-35, 37, 79
Coelophysis 30-31
Compsognathus 26-27
crocodiles 35, 38, 42
Cryptoclidus 88-89

**D**
Deinonychus 32-33
Deinosuchus 42-43
Dimorphodon 72-73
Diplodocus 48-49
Dsungaripterus 70-71

**E**
eggs 16-17, 40, 85
Elasmosaurus 82-83
Eoraptor 28-29
Eudimorphodon 66-67

**F**
feathers 36, 40, 67, 78-79
flying reptiles 14, 66-67, 68-69, 70-71, 72-73, 74-75, 76-77, 78-79
food 12-13, 15
footprints 7, 73
fossils 6-7, 8-9, 10-11, 21, 25, 27, 30, 36, 40, 46, 51, 56, 63, 70, 76, 86, 88, 91, 93

**G**
Giganotosaurus 24-25

**H**
Hadrosaurus 44-45
herbivores 8, 12 (and see plant-eaters)
Heterodontosaurus 64-65
horns 58, 60
Hypsilophodon 8-9, 10-11

**I**
ichthyosaurs 86, 91
Ichthyosaurus 84-85
Iguanodon 56-57
insects 27, 29, 37, 68, 78

**J**
jaws 35, 41, 71, 75, 78

**K**
Kronosaurus 80-81

**L**
Liopleurodon 90-91
lizards 27, 29, 38, 68, 93

**M**
meat-eaters 12-13, 15, 18-19, 20-21, 22-23, 24-25, 26-27, 28-29, 30-31, 32-33, 34-35, 36-37, 38-39, 40-41, 42-43, 66-67, 68-69, 70-71, 72-73, 74-75, 76-77, 78-79, 80-81, 82-83, 84-85, 86-87, 88-89, 90-91, 92-93
mosasaurs 92-93
mother dinosaurs 18

**O**
Oviraptor 40-41

**P**
plant-eaters 8, 12, 19, 20, 38, 44-45, 46-47, 48-49, 50-51, 52-53, 54-55, 56-57, 58-59, 60-61, 62-63, 64-65

Plateosaurus 46-47
plates 50-51
plesiosaurs 88, 90-91
Pterodactylus 68-69
pterosaurs 68-69, 70, 72, 76

**Q**
Quetzalcoatlus 74-75

**R**
reptiles 14-15, 17, 38

**S**
Sauropelta 52-53
sauropods 48
Sauroposeidon 62-63
scientists 6-7, 11, 21, 25, 27, 30, 32-33, 36-37, 40, 46, 51, 56, 60, 63, 72-73, 75, 76, 78, 86, 88, 91
Segnosaurus 36-37
Shonisaurus 86-87
Sordes 76-77
spikes 50, 53
Stegosaurus 50-51
Stygimoloch 60-61
Suchomimus 34-35
swimming reptiles 15, 80-81, 82-83, 84-85, 86-87, 88-89, 90-91, 92-93

**T**
tails 27, 43, 45, 49, 54, 66, 76, 84, 92
teeth 7, 13, 20, 25, 41, 44, 53, 64, 67, 71, 78, 81, 83, 87, 89, 91
Triceratops 18, 58-59
Tylosaurus 92-93
Tyrannosaurus rex 7, 22-23, 24, 28

**W**
wings 14, 40, 66, 69, 74-75, 76-77, 79